SYLLABLES GO BY

SIXTEEN HUNDRED EIGHTY-THREE
THREE LINES AT A TIME

BY SONNY BREWER

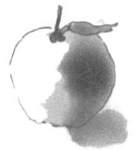

SYLLABLES GO BY

SIXTEEN HUNDRED EIGHTY–THREE
THREE LINES AT A TIME

BY SONNY BREWER

OVER THE TRANSOM PUBLISHING (WBP)

OVER THE TRANSOM PUBLISHING (WBP)

Waterhole Branch Productions
10930 Sandy Lane
Waterhole Branch, Alabama 36532

Sonny@SonnyBrewer.com

Copyright © by Sonny Brewer 2020

ISBN 13: 9780578638119
ISBN: 978-0-578-63811-9

No part of this work may be reproduced or distributed without permission of the author.

This book was designed
by my dear, sweet friend,
Dorothy Carico Smith

caricosmith.com
caricosmith1@mac.com

*This book is dedicated to the belief that
Love is the First Cause and
Organizing Principle of the Cosmos*

FOREWORD

WHEN I DRANK whisky, I drank Scotch whisky. Blended. Dewar's by name. Friends would sometimes present me with a gift of expensive single malt scotch, and I would share it with other friends while pouring into my own glass from a bottle of Dewar's. I prefer things that are blended.

I like my religion blended, too. Born to a Baptist mama, from there I added some Presbyterian because I like Scotch whisky and bagpipe music and the idea of wearing kilts. I wanted to be a Quaker, and went on Sunday mornings to the Fairhope Friends Meeting house for a couple of years. I'm a reading fan of Buddhism, Taoism and Sufism. Now and then I've sat in a pew during Christian Science and Unitarian Universalist services. I've joined in on covered dish potluck home gatherings of the local Baha'i Faith. During my Methodist period I applied and was accepted to seminary then changed my mind and didn't enroll; but, I did preach a Methodist funeral a few weeks ago. I'm a cardholding Catholic who defected to the Episcopal Church for five years. And, these days I'm not going to church in buildings. Except last week when I took a notion to go to a Unity Church service when I was in Tuscaloosa to visit my sister.

I also like a blended literary experience. Stephen King's writing and Cormac McCarthy's, some Tolstoy and some James Lee Burke. Same with philosophy and music and art and politics. And—well, the point is made.

These little poems, then, are themselves a blend, my own personal take on the Japanese haiku form. For one thing, a haiku is supposed to give Mother Nature a role, mention plants or animals, celestial bodies, the weather, lakes or rivers. In some of these I do, and in some I do not.

A Japanese haiku is a three-line poem having seventeen syllables. The rule for the pattern itself makes a whimsical haiku.

> Five in the first line
> seven in the second line
> five in the third line

This scheme of lines and syllables I have adhered to. When you mix narrative with haiku, as I've done in this collection, it becomes haibun, a name made up in the seventeenth century by Matsuo Basho, Japan's haiku master, whose best hits (from the *Narrow Road to the Interior* translation into English by Sam Hamill) always include:

> An old silent pond…
>
> A frog jumps into the pond,
>
> splash! Silence again

Another one that I like, though I don't quite get the last line. Which is part of the fun.

> Why, just this autumn
> I have suddenly grown old—
> a bird in the clouds

An example from Basho where there is no mention of nature. Also, there are only four syllables in the last line, in both the English translation as well as the Japanese original: *daiku kana.*

> Year-end housekeeping—
>
> hanging his own shelf at last,
>
> the carpenter

And, one more from brother Basho. Notice how he kind of fudges the syllable count by borrowing one from the second line and loaning it to the first, the master himself playing around with the form.

> A rolling cloud—like
>
> a dog pissing on the run—
>
> dense winter showers

A child can write a haiku, and, indeed, I was first introduced to the form when I was a kid. Simplicity is another charm of the little poems.

But, haiku can be also taken to the level of art as Basho and others have done.

Below the level of art and Basho's genius, I am here keeping it playful—like the title together with the subtitle is a haiku—while also writing seriously, especially about matters of the spirit and my faith.

Finally, because of a thing I have with nines, I include in this book ninety-nine spare poems that are images of my thoughts in seventeen syllables. If only one of them works for you, then I am grateful and blessed.

Sonny Brewer
Waterhole Branch, Alabama

MY LITTLE DOG Bobby jumps on the bed and curls up in a sleepy ball, hardly budging when I brush against an apple on the counter with my arm. It falls and bounces at my feet then rolls across the kitchen floor. This pup, gentle cousin to the hungry wolf, is at ease indoors and content to be just where he is. Or is he?

ONE

Little dog sleeps late
upon his master's pillow—
dreaming daylight hunts

THERE ARE STORIES of devoted dogs who mourn the death of their masters. Sometimes taking up a vigil at their graves, deeply aware of their absence, and something missing from their hearts. I wonder, might an animal also have a sense of loss soon to come?

Two

Christ on a donkey,
Palm fronds waved for him up high—
the small, sad beast weeps

THERE IS VAST energy and motion in love, a background of singular intention that is sometimes rendered in tiny, subtle moments.

THREE

Water's blue green deeps
go rolling toward the seashore
planting sand kisses

EMERSON, ON THE intoxication of travel, wrote some hundred and fifty years ago of his surprise to find someone well-known waiting for him there at his destination in a foreign land—himself. "My giant goes with me wherever I go," he said. So, we might as well be at ease with where we are, since that's the only place we can be.

FOUR

Apple rolls downhill,
finds a hole and lies stock still,
pleased to be at home

WHEN JESUS ASKED us not to worry, because he had overcome the sorrows of this world, and, further, that the things he did we can also do, it seems to me he was talking about the common origin we share with him in the mystery of creation. He said in the book of John that he is actually in us.

There is one life. It is not doled out separately to humans, the myriad beasts, birds, and plants. Even fire breathes the life-breath that rises up from the ground of our mutual being, from our very souls, untouched by Shakespeare's "… heart-ache, and the thousand natural shocks that flesh is heir to."

FIVE

Spanish moss shivers,
cold wind blows through the oak trees—
roots lie still and dark

I READ ON the Wikipedia site, that "if a story has a character arc, the character begins as one sort of person and gradually transforms into a different sort of person in response to changing developments in the story."

And I read here in my heart that we shall all come around to our best selves, maybe in the twinkling of an eye, or maybe over millennia, but we prodigals, all of us, have a welcome waiting.

Six

Waves wind-born at sea,
Mother Ocean sets them free—
sun turns them to sky

AS PER ORIGINAL design, balance, alignment, measure, equality, and perfection.

SEVEN

Bird's wing on the left,
another on its right side—
juxtaposition!

MY LITTLE DOG Bobby explores his world. His curiosity is as pretty as a flower blooming in spring. Some things, however, he seems to know as if reading from his DNA scheme.

Here around my cabin, in these woods along the banks of Waterhole Branch, I don't strap a collar around his neck. He's not on a leash. I keep an eye on him.

When the owl called at twilight, I could see Bobby down the hill, fifty yards away.

The barred owls who live in the neighborhood have a wing span of maybe five feet. Suddenly, I wondered could such an owl take flight with my puppy. I was about to whistle him home, when Bobby settled the issue all on his own.

EIGHT

Sing, Who cooks for you?
Barred owl's voice from a branch—
little dog runs home

I DIDN'T DISCOVER the thing with 9s. It was told to me by a teacher in college.

The math teacher explained that the sum of the digits of a number is called the *digital root* of that number. It simply means adding together numbers until you come up with a single digit. Say, 346257. 3+4+6+2+5+7=27, and 2+7=9.

Now, she said, do the multiplication tables with a 9—times *any* number. The digital root of the product always adds up to a 9. Try it.

What boggles my mind even more is that it works with 99, or 999, or 9999…times any number has a digital root of 9.

Crazier still, to me, is if either of two multipliers has a digital root of 9, the product has a digital root of 9. Like 72x3=216, and 2+1+6=9. Or, 324x902=292,248, and (yes) those numbers add to 27, which reduces to 9.

It doesn't work that way with any other number. Not 2s, 3s, 4s, 5s, 6s, 7s, or 8s.

9s have shown up in my life in meaningful ways. The address of my Over the Transom Bookstore was 9 North Church Street. I founded a nonprofit called the Fairhope Center for Writing Arts, and later came up with a little bungalow to use as a retreat for writers-in-residence. The address of the Wolff Writers' Cottage is 9 North School Street. When many years ago I rented a post office box in Fairhope, I was randomly assigned 639. The list goes on.

I also love the shape of a 9. Make a big 9 with your finger in the air. Do a single line starting with the tail, or start with the head. See?

So, of course, I decided to include 99 poems in this chapbook. With each having 17 syllables, that's a thousand, six hundred and eighty-three syllables, of which number the digital root is 9. I'm not a math head. But, I have a math *heart* for 9s.

NINE

There's a thing with 9s
I don't really understand—
products summed, still 9s

DAG HAMMARSKJOLD IS counted by some as a modern mystic, but his day job was Secretary General of the United Nations from 1953 to 1961. He died in that office at the age of 56, killed in a plane crash on his way to cease-fire negotiations during the Congo Crisis.

He kept a journal that was published posthumously as *Markings*. In the year he died, on Whitsunday, he wrote in his journal, "I don't know Who—or What—put the question, I don't know when it was put. I don't even remember answering. But at some moment I did answer Yes to Someone—or Something—and from that hour I was certain that existence is meaningful and that, therefore, my life, in self-surrender, had a goal."

TEN

Possibilities
finding purchase in a yes—
sun and rain on fields

PERCEPTION IS THE root of all and everything in this world. Judgment born of perception lacks knowledge that only God has. When we cease to judge, this world is overcome.

ELEVEN

Rooster eats at dawn,
owl gets his breakfast at dusk—
Sunday brunch for me

IF YOU'RE FOLLOWING the flight of a bumblebee during the Sermon on the Mount, you'll be distracted and miss the finer points of the talk. Instead of the beauty of hearing it live, you'll have to catch the as-told-to version. That one degree of separation is where the trouble starts.

TWELVE

The advice, my son—

fathers, priests, all say the same—

have ears to hear now

WE TALK A lot about the weather. The weather pays us no mind. But when we *listen* to the weather, there are songs and stories to hear.

THIRTEEN

Rain falls on the roof,
a mother's sweet lullaby—
thunder shakes the crib

WHEREVER I GO, there I am. Still, sometimes, there are places I would rather be.

FOURTEEN

It's cold in my house,
it's soft and warm in my bed—
I sigh and get up

WISDOM ADVISES US to take no thought for tomorrow. For one thing, it'll never come. Wisdom's advice, on the other hand, is based on yesterday, and neither does that day exist. Go ahead, try to do something yesterday.

FIFTEEN

Tick-tock, clock, tick-tock,
we have ears to hear the gears—
time's convincing trick

IT IS SAID that we live forever in our children.

Sixteen

Ashes and ashes,

Mom and Dad rest side-by-side—

kids are at the beach.

A DOG CAN'T TALK to its doctor, nor understand the prognosis. But it knows what it knows.

SEVENTEEN

Puppy's nose is wet,
a good sign the doctor says—
little dog sneezes!

CLOUDY PUFFBALLS FORM a pattern like fish scales scattered across the sky and promise a change in the weather. Meteorologists know why sailor's sayings are true, why a red sky at night is a delight, and at morning it's a warning.

My grandmother was neither a sailor nor a weather girl on the television, and yet she understood things the sky had to say. She'd not even stop sweeping the front porch as she let us in on what was coming our way.

EIGHTEEN

Pale moon, thin halo
catches a single bright star—
tomorrow it rains

BIRDS AND BABIES, fires and floods, tornadoes and roses, arise from a common creative impulse. If instead of skin and feathers we could see the life urge in all of creation, see life's uncreated light, if the self-organizing principle, or breath itself had color and hue, or love made some sound that we could hum for a few bars, forgiveness would be a piece of cake.

NINETEEN

One life arises

in each of us as brothers—

"fame and shame the same"

MY LITTLE DOG Bobby was once such a valiant hunting dog before he became the cultured canine who now goes with me to the bookstore and coffeehouse. He seems to have totally forgot his early childhood in the woods.

TWENTY

Footfall on dry leaves
wakes up the dozing squirrel—
little dog walks away

Some who have eyes and ears for nature's mysteries become our teachers, our poets and prophets.

TWENTY-ONE

Old oak tells secrets,
Thoreau listened carefully—
we ask what's for lunch

WHEN I WAS DOING business at Over the Transom Books I sold used and rare books, and a few new novels by contemporary Southern writers, mostly the work of people I knew. I'd unlock the door on quiet mornings and even in the empty store, the company of so many books was like walking into a parlor filled with guests sharing stories. Kind of noisy. With a smoky scent of age in the room, pleasant, like a favorite tweed jacket. I get the same feeling of companionship now that I'm a writer and have the pleasure of sitting near books that are themselves inspiration, like the promise of rain in a dry season.

TWENTY-TWO

Study lined with books,
desk, lamp, paper, ink and pen—
words drop from cloud forms

I DON'T HOLD my heat so well anymore, as the old folks say.

And yet.

Driving down the road the day before Christmas, I saw up ahead a rotund, balding man who was somewhere north of 60 years old, strolling out to his mailbox wearing shorts, rubber shower shoes, an open Hawaiian shirt layered over a wife-beater. It was in the low 40s. He threw up his hand, smiling at me as I passed like I was an old pal, and let's head to the beach.

And it occurred to me that maybe what's hot and what's cold is all a matter of attitude.

TWENTY-THREE

A knock at the door,
winter wind rushes inside
for a fireside chat

TWENTY-FOUR

Gray and foggy morning,
cold clouds settled on wet ground—
coffee warms my cup

TWENTY FIVE

Cold snap turns the leaves,
frogs and lizards burrow down—
chimney warms the moon

THE COUPLE WERE seated opposite each other in a cafe booth. The man and woman had cell phones in their hands, in front of their faces. They stared expressionless at their screens, thumbs poised, thumbs typing, a thousand miles away from the real-time moment in the cafe. I let the scene dissolve and come back into focus on them sitting shoulder-to-shoulder, sharing one Samsung Galaxy between them, laughing at a family video posted on Facebook.

TWENTY-SIX

Old woman, old man,
sitting knee-to-knee in chairs—
both of them asleep

THE BEST-SELLING poet in the United States is a man from Persia who died about seven hundred and fifty years ago. He was a Sufi mystic with a really long name, but most people simply call him Rumi.

Read from *A Year with Rumi* edited by Coleman Barks and see why he's such a big hit these centuries later. Rumi wrote this line, "Today, like every other day, we wake up empty and frightened. Don't open the door to the study and begin reading. Take down the dulcimer…"

And I get it. While sleeping and dreaming, and upon first waking in this world with what we know about it, there's an almost reflexive response to sigh. But if we'll stop our minds with bookish big ideas for a minute, sort of reboot with some basic gratitude for another new morning's chance at loving, smiling, and something beautiful, then the day is recovered for some wonder.

TWENTY-SEVEN

Now I wake me up,
dreams recede into cool dark—
light changes everything

'TWAS THE 28TH day of January, 1949, a bone cold morning just before daylight in Lamar County, Alabama, and a seventeen-year-old girl bore down and pushed me into my story.

TWENTY-EIGHT

On a feather bed
in my grandfather's farmhouse—
turn to the first page

NATURE IS ALWAYS interesting in her contradictions. Sort of like a handsome man or a beautiful woman, with one brown eye and one blue eye.

TWENTY-NINE

Lightning splits the sky,
earth and air caught in the burn—
long night still and cold

I HEARD A story about a man who went away on a business trip. He told his family he would be back on Friday. He finished his work early and decided he'd walk in unannounced and surprise his wife and kids. He had done this before over the years and he loved the way his children reacted with such joy to see him.

When he quietly opened the door, patted the dog on the head, and slipped inside, he found supper waiting and everyone seated. His place was set at the head of the table, all eyes on him, smiles all around. The dog had two hours ago taken up her spot by the front door, nose and eyes toward the door knob, the way she always greeted him. She hadn't done that on the other days of his absence. They knew this would be another sneak-in.

And, if it *ever* happens that a dog, or your odd Aunt Lucy, has some accurate prescient knowledge, that means foreknowledge is a doable deal. Even if the rest of us don't all yet know how to do it. In fact, one instance of *anything* by *anyone* opens a door to all of us. Like, say, some one person actually loving his neighbors as himself.

THIRTY

Only one white crow
proves that all crows are not black,
said William James

PERCEPTION DOES NOT issue forth from fact, rather it relies on opinion we picked up down some yesterday road. Maybe in Mama's kitchen.

THIRTY-ONE

Stand back from the stove,
a watched pot never boils—
water knows better

I WALKED MY Little Dog Bobby outside on a foggy, moonless night. A reflection from the porchlight echoed off the wet grass at my feet, revealing fallen stars.

THIRTY-TWO

Fog enshrouds the night,
cold damp breath blows away stars—
crystal dewdrops shine

SOMETIMES, THE THING of our interest that has our attention has no interest in our attention.

THIRTY-THREE

Artist concentrates,

eyes and hand working as one—

apples in a bowl

I LAY BACK on a gentle grassy slope, thinking to close my eyes on the world for a breath or two. But a speck winging across the sky, way up high, teased me to follow the bird—maybe a crow—out of sight. And I imagined how the world must appear from so far above it all.

THIRTY-FOUR

Full moon peeks through clouds,
yellow eye surveys the world—
birds sleep on their roost

I HAVE A gold pocket watch and chain that belonged to my father. It's a Waltham railroad watch with a smaller inset dial on the face for the second hand. It's a beautiful vintage timepiece that he won in a poker game in Fairbanks, Alaska. He gave it to his father, with HAPPY BIRTHDAY DAD inscribed on the back.

When Pop Brewer died, Daddy took it back. When Daddy died, I got it.

When it stopped working I snapped the gold chain clasp to the twist switch on a tall lamp that sits on my desk beside the computer. I'm looking at the watch now. I dangled it there to remind myself to take it the repair shop. It's been hanging there for almost a year. I decided to leave the hands paused just where they are.

Sort of a reminder of the reality of time, and how the Dalai Lama speaks of time. He said there are two days in the year when nothing can be done, *yesterday* and *tomorrow*. Now, he went on, is the only moment for action, for loving and kindness.

THIRTY-FIVE

Clocks may ratchet 'round—
time's hands do not move at all—
it's raining right now

ONE YEAR FOR the observance of Lent, I gave up reading. That was hard. Another year, I gave up watermelon. That was not hard. Watermelons are not available until the summer.

When once I sat in a pew and listened to a sermon about Lenten sacrifice, I wondered what the priest might himself have in mind.

Thirty-Six

Forty days of Lent
replicates the sacrifice—
Adam gives up apples

EVEN AS A kid dragged off to church, mad about tight shoes and a tucked shirt, I was still able to pick up a few things the preacher said. But you know how sullen little boys are. In such a rotten mood, I'd find something wrong with a cone of vanilla. Make it chocolate, or just keep your ice cream.

Now my reference is low key and laidback, rarely in a mood. I'm no longer a churchgoer, but I still know some Bible verses. Some of them, to me, still sound like misquotes.

THIRTY-SEVEN

Because He loves us,
not the other way around,
all things work for good

I'VE WORKED HEAVY construction. Walked through a gate onto a steel and concrete landscape of cranes, buckhoists, scaffolding, concrete forms, track hoes and big trucks. Worn a hardhat and steel toe boots, earplugs for the jackhammers, facemasks for the dust. Skin and shirt and pants got grimy. Workers everywhere, watchful for something falling, cautious for trip hazards.

Plumbers, electricians, frame and drywall crews, welders, tile men and flooring crews, painters—men and some women on the move, hustling all over a job site. Chattering, telling stories, laughing and cursing. Bending their backs making a building come out of the ground.

And, then sometimes, I imagine great and beautiful things created from thought and impulse without stones or steel, hammers or muscles.

THIRTY-EIGHT

Listen for silence,
God's bright calm causing the world—
shout hallelujah!

RUPERT SHELDRAKE HAS been known to attack scientific and intellectual orthodoxy. He's a British scientist, Cambridge-trained biochemist and plant physiologist. He wonders whether or not the sun—or for that matter, I suppose, a hurricane or volcano—is conscious. He thinks so. He can use Greek and Roman mythology and science way over my head to make his convincing case.

I once had a brand new Martin guitar, and the brochure promised that as I played my new guitar the molecules in the wood would respond and reposition themselves in a unique way according to the way I strummed and picked, its contact with my arms and legs and my belly, my fingers on the fretboard. My Martin would become like no other Martin guitar in existence. It would, according to the guitar makers, become an instrument that was an extension of my consciousness.

And if wood can *respond* to consciousness, might it not also *possess* consciousness?

A friend said of My Little Dog Bobby, "It's just a dog." I don't agree.

And wood's not just wood.

THIRTY-NINE

>Little dog sleeping,
>see him breathe the tide of life,
>dreaming creation

THEORETICAL PHYSICIST STEPHEN Hawking said the formula for creation is complete without the need for God. "It is not necessary to invoke God to light the [fuse] and set the universe going," he said. God's not needed, according to Hawking, to write a mathematical description of reality, or to prove a Unified Field theory.

Hawking also said, "I regard the brain as a computer which will stop working when its components fail. There is no heaven or afterlife for broken-down computers; that is a fairy story for people afraid of the dark." And yet.

Hawking was diagnosed with ALS and given, at most, three years to live. He was 21. Then when he got married, he said it gave him "something to live for." The companionship of a woman made him want to live. He and Jane Wilde had three children.

And he didn't didn't follow doctor's orders. He lived to 76. Mostly he was crumpled in a wheelchair and spoke through a voice simulator. But when he was 65, he took a flight in a 727 to experience weightlessness. "I want to show that people need not be limited by physical handicaps as long as they are not disabled in spirit."

Dr. Hawking wrote formulas for black holes and cosmic events. But, there's no equation for *love* and *companionship*, for *spirit*, the stuff that makes life worth living. Subtle consciousness is not a mathematical, theoretical concept for the chalkboards. Sort of like God, Who *is* Himself the Unified Field.

FORTY

> Where are the numbers
> when flows the rolling cadence
> of love's mysteries

BLAISE PASCAL, 17TH century French mathematician and philosopher, said all the problems of humankind can be traced to our inability to sit quietly, alone in a room with nothing at all to do.

Maybe all that moving around does lead to trouble.

FORTY-ONE

Apples have no legs—
spiders have four on a side
and sometimes bite you

IN THE BLEAK cold of a damp and gray winter's day, an old man's fancy lightly turns to thoughts of warmer days, wondering of the sun, Why hast thou forsaken me?

FORTY-TWO

In my winter dreams
there are worlds far lovelier—
stroll through summer rain

AND YET. WHEN those summer days sweat the air and make it close and thick and the sun is blistering hot for weeks on end, I sing a different song.

FORTY-THREE

Sense of the seasons,

the sun keeping careful track—

I dream of autumn

WHEN I WAS a college boy, I was assigned to read Truman Capote's *Other Voices, Other Rooms*. I didn't like it, and I didn't finish it.

Years later I saw Capote on the *Tonight Show* with Johnny Carson, who asked him which of his books was his favorite. Without pause, Capote said, *Other Voices, Other Rooms*. Hmm?

So, I had another go at it and couldn't put it down. The book had not changed. I was, however, a different man.

Ralph Waldo Emerson said that a man is a "collecting principle unto himself." Like, if two people stretched their nets across the river of life, one would catch and keep some stuff the other would throw away. "Dude, I can't believe you threw away that piece of flotsam, that scrap of jetsam!"

When I was a Baptist boy, I was required to read parts of the Bible. Even memorize verses. I didn't like it and didn't find much to keep. I couldn't wait to fold my net and go home.

FORTY-FOUR

Book I can't put down
was one day just a spacer
between two novels

JESUS AND BUDDHA had something huge and important in common. Jesus did not write down anything. And. Buddha did not write down anything. I cannot imagine.

Forty-Five

Fumbling and awkward
trying to learn Jesus-words—
words He didn't write

Forty-Six

And if I'd been born
over there not *over here*,
what would Buddha do?

I'M GLAD THERE are those who had an aching urge to write about these two men and what they talked about, the teachings they left us, their pathways to peace.

Forty-Seven

Unsayable things,
if left unsaid for too long,
rivers will run dry

WRITERS ALWAYS, HOWEVER, put their own autobiographical spin on the words and lines they write. They cannot do otherwise.

FORTY-EIGHT

Left alone to hear
strange suggestions from my heart—
I'll translate for you

FoLK RoCK DUo the Indigo Girls had lines in a song, "I gotta get out of bed and get a hammer and a nail / learn how to use my hands / not just my head / I think myself into jail…".

In my novel *The Poet of Tolstoy Park*, I wrote about the main character Henry Stuart spending time at a spiritual retreat. And the priest in charge required everyone to check in their books and journals. Like leaving your guns at the door in an Old West saloon, the priest believed it would keep everyone out of trouble. Henry and the others had to grab shovels and axes and rakes. For the entire stay at the retreat, everybody had to dig and chop and rake.

FORTY-NINE

Let me roll the cart,
not try to invent the wheel—
thinking's too much work

I read a piece about some of the physiological things that happen when you lock eyes with someone. And especially, across the room with someone of the opposite sex whom you do not know. Something like magic bubbles inside our minds and bodies, chemicals and responses that can be measured.

In the reporting, there was also a brief paragraph about finding yourself *regarded* in a stare by an animal at the zoo. You are being considered, thought about, responded to by an animal who cannot speak to you, but whose thoughts are captured by you, whose thoughts are directed toward you.

I have a little dog Bobby. Looking at Bobby, who seems to be always looking at me, must be something like gazing at God. You find Him always gazing right back at you through a window you left open.

FIFTY

Mighty soulful stare,
he looks straight into my eyes
looking back at him

FITY-ONE

Gazing into eyes—
iris, pupil, how they change—
silent soul unchanged

oNE VERSE IN scripture that gives me pause is Jesus quoted in John 14:20 saying, "On that day you shall know that I am in my Father, and you are in me, and I am in you."

I used to believe Jesus meant when I'm dead I'd see things clearly.

Now I believe "On that day..." is *any* day I'm transformed by some renewal of my mind.

FIFTY-TWO

This day makes more sense—
there'd be nothing left *that day*
to know You're in me

FIFTY-THREE

> John fourteen twenty:
> I in Him in me in you—
> sweet entanglement*

*From Wikipedia: Quantum *entanglement* is a physical phenomenon which occurs when pairs or groups of particles…cannot be described independently of the state of the other(s), even when the particles *are separated by a large distance…*

This ability of one thing to have a physical effect on another thing without them touching, Albert Einstein called "spooky action at a distance." It would be like watching a game of pool where a shot on one table moves a ball on another table. Pretty holy ghostly.

ITTS HARD TO be an animal these days. So many roads to cross with so many cars going so fast. Even if creatures do have this uncanny ability to cross at right angles, never running a long diagonal to get to the other side of the road, they still have it rough.

Then there's the one about the slowest of them all catching a big break.

FIFTY-FOUR

Making funny sounds,
pickup truck chugs to a stop—
turtle crosses road

WITH A SUPER power called omniscience, He had to know we'd mess this place up.

And yet.

FIFTY-FIVE

In the beginning,
God's odd intention to love
what shall come undone

NEAR THE MIDDLE of the month in January of 2019 there was a *super blood wolf moon*. A super moon is one that appears larger, and because it's in the perigee of its orbit around earth, it actually is closer. And, a blood moon is a moon in total eclipse that turns a rusty red color.

These two things happened on the same night.

Plus, because it was a January full moon, it's nicknamed a wolf moon from olden times when ancient families were taunted by the nighttime howling of hungry wolves on the frozen perimeter of their village.

One of the players in an eclipse drama is light that is, of course, eternally present. Less conspicuous, but just as necessary is the shadow that is also always there beyond our earth.

Hold this image in mind: earth has a shadow (even when the moon doesn't prove it), a tubular shaft of darkness extending always deep into space. It goes almost a million miles. Past that earth's *umbra* sort of fades away in an outer space night that's darker than a shadow.

FIFTY-SIX

Long shadows at night,
pouring blood on a full moon—
wolves cry in answer

I HAD A friend Paul Bell who loved to say on those many rainy days in Mobile, Alabama, where he lived, that people ought not complain about a downpour. "Rain's water and water's life," he'd say.

In 1981 in Belfast, Northern Ireland, inmates at Maze Prison went on a hunger strike. Ten men died between 45 and 61 days without food. Without water, death would have come in as few as three days. But the sweetness of life demanded at least some brief stay.

FIFTY-SEVEN

Rain is cool water
and quenches blind thirst for life,
a gift sweet and pure

AND SOMETIMES, BUT rarely, life is given up for some greater good, and that passion is a message written in love's best portion and sets a watermark on human history.

FIFTY-EIGHT

Drifting down, down, down,
a dying oak leaf falling,
lands red, yellow, gold

Some days, without warning, there is a fullness of mind and spirit, that makes everything smell better, look better, sound better, taste better, and feel better. Our senses are bright and intense and if we could bottle it up, we'd want to stay drunk on the experience.

FIFTY-NINE

A state of Grace comes
from where I don't know, nor how,
else I'd follow close

TURNS OUT, HOWEVER, we can, if we reach down deep, pour from a bottle of inner peace. MRIs and EEGs prove actual changes in the way we think after meditation.

The practice of meditation makes it all better.

Look into Centering Prayer as meditation from Father Thomas Keating; the Jesus Prayer from the Orthodox Christian tradition; Mindfulness meditation; Transcendental Meditation. All meditation, including praying the rosary, is about finding in the depth of our consciousness that "inner room" (Matthew 6:6) where there is silence, stillness, and calm—and a small, still voice for love and forgiveness.

I HAVE A friend who is rich and almost a hundred years old. I dedicated my novel *The Poet of Tolstoy Park* to Ray, who lived aboard his 42-foot Hinckley sailboat here in Fairhope. He was my guru, preacher-man, and best friend.

Ray told me many things that helped me to see differently.

Like, if a thing will have no value a million years from now, he said, it has no value now, none at all. I mentioned Shelley's poem *Ozymandias*. Ray asked me to find a copy and bring it to the boat, he'd love to read it again. I did. He read the poem aloud to us both, and as his words took purchase it was plain to see that only love in action has value a million years from now.

ONE MORNING, WITH a fat pelican on a piling next to the boat cocking its eye toward me, I asked Ray what was his most valuable possession?" Without hesitation he answered, "My mind's ability to experience insight. An insight is an incredible thing. Forever valuable."

Then he said this world is an illusion of individual perceptions that block insight. "Some people think a Hinckley is the best sailboat in the world. But not the man who owns a Swan."

Ray's sailboat was named *Illusion*, lettered in real gold leaf in a graceful arc on that pretty wineglass transom.

Sixty

Moments of insight—
illusions vanish like dreams
when I awaken

I WATCH MY little dog Bobby as he falls asleep, and I know from my dog book that his heart rate will slow and his blood pressure will drop. Then, in about ten minutes he'll enter REM sleep, and "dream like humans." That's right out of the book. And, since I know that he loves to bother squirrels, I guess that's mostly what he dreams about.

Sixty-one

Little dog's heart slows,
then races in some dreamscape
for squirrels—or me

ALL OF MY perceptions are constructed and maintained entirely by personal preferences and my own past experience. But I often hope for seeing that's not so lopsided.

Like, when I look at you, if I couldn't see you, maybe I'd see you better.

Sixty-Two

Love sees all while blind,
unknown to not-this not-that—
no degrees or kinds

Sixty-Three

Love is like itself,
undivided, outside time—
its rhythm, its rhyme

Sixty-Four

Love counts one as all—
moments in eternity
rise upon the fall

OFTEN, IN THE mornings I go outside, and do a little Tai Chi blended with some Qigong exercise and self-styled yoga. I stay out of sight of the neighbors.

So I was dismayed to one day get a text message from my son in Colorado who said a friend of his (the visiting granddaughter of my neighbor) saw me doing some funny movements on the lawn and took a photo and sent to him.

From now on, I'll keep behind a big palmetto palm. A few days later, however, I do wish I had photo evidence of this very strange thing that happened. I've told maybe a dozen people. I'm not convinced they believe me.

It was a sparrow, and it actually paced around up there. Its little feet were cold on my bald head. Then, when I uttered an uncontrollable loudish whisper—Wow!—it flew into a palmetto palm right beside be.

I looked at him. He looked at me. And flew away.

Sixty-Five

Tai Chi on the ridge—
monkey steps back, stork spreads wings—
bird lands on my head

I CAN BE hypnotized by a great blue heron wading in the water, it's movements so very slow and deliberate, like silence in motion. And there is often a heron who visits this stretch of Waterhole Branch.

I usually see him—it has to be a male because he is so huge—somewhere along the very same 30-yard bend in the creek.

Then one evening when the sun and sky were magnificent together, blue palette and flaming pigment, with night already coming out of the ground low in the underbrush, the giant heron glided overhead, not even a whisper from his wings. He was just high enough above the trees to catch the sun's yellow beams streaming through the live oaks.

Sixty-Six

Autumn gold twilight,
great blue heron flies overhead
silent wings on fire

THE GREEN ALCHEMY that trees share is a miracle of oxygen-brewing that keeps us alive and breathing. Trees of the deciduous brethren abandon their good work in the fall and through a sleepy winter.

But here in this damp subtropical land of backwater branches and swampy lagoons, the evergreen sorcerers are a clear majority. What's not so common is to find three different species clumped together, only two of them wearing the jade, all crowded into a single bundle on a point jutting out into Waterhole Branch.

It's probably a holy spot of ground.

Sixty-Seven

Juniper is green,
magnolia cloaked the same—
gray oak still napping

IT WAS A Kodak moment (do people still know what that means?) when a little green tree frog showed up to join all the bugs gathered in the lamplight shining through to the outside of my picture window.

I expected him to just hop all over the place, enjoying a smorgasbord of crunchy critters.

I was wrong. He was a perfect student of The Tao and sat completely still, and let his supper come to him.

Sixty-Eight

Window light draws bugs—
little green tree frog joins in,
toes still, mouth spread wide

I'VE COME UP with a mindfulness meditation technique that helps me to hold on to the clarity of right now. It's the same trick I use for curing hiccups that has not failed me yet, including on other people.

I don't really get the phrase *mindfulness meditation*. It seems to me a contradiction, since meditation serves to ground us in the holy instant, and leave our minds empty, not full.

Anyway, my cure for hiccups. I focus my imagination on a hiccup rising like a bubble to the surface of some placid crystal lake. In my mind's eye, I see the water's surface undisturbed. I focus my concentration, and wait for the next bubble to bloop to the surface. That's it. No more hiccups. Sort of like that watched pot never boils.

I am able to return my mind to the emptiness of now in the same way. Except the bubble I'm waiting for is not a hiccup, but *my next thought*. If I direct and concentrate my attention on the *origin* of my next thought, it takes a longer time for a thought to originate, and that interval is a space of silence. It doesn't last long.

But, as I keep practicing, I have longer periods of stillness.

Sixty-Nine

> How to still your mind—
> close your eyes to watch thoughts born,
> behold their refrain

Seventy

> Wind blows away grace,
> stillness fetches it back home—
> hold open the door

And in the deep place of quiet, surprises emerge.

Seventy-One

> I thought I forgot,
> and then I remembered You
> Whose name I don't know

HENRY DAVID THOREAU loved the outside, and not as a spectator. He chose to participate rather than just looking around. Thoreau suggested that it's one thing to be called outside to see a full moon, and another thing entirely to find your way through the forest along a path lighted only by the moon.

I walk My Little Dog Bobby outside every night just before bedtime, and one deep dark night I was delighted to learn that a spider's eyes, if it is looking straight at you, will bounce back to you the light from your flashlight. Out of doors—that's where the magic lies.

SEVENTY-TWO

Diamond, or dew?
my flashlight across the grass—
spider laughing, looks at me

And now and then, what's *out there* comes *in here*

.

SEVENTY-THREE

Someone opened the door,
the world outside wild and green—
tree frog in my chair

IN JAPANESE CULTURE, the principle of Wabi-sabi teaches that beauty and value are present in things that are not perfect. In fact, there are even Kintsugi masters who follow a centuries-old practice of repairing broken pottery with powdered gold, silver, and platinum mixed with lacquer. So the cracks are transformed to seams of rare and precious beauty. Flaws are not hidden.

I use plain old Elmer's glue to put back together coffee cups and cereal bowls. I don't have shiny stuff to stir into my glue. But when it's dark inside my house and a big round moon shines its light onto the long-necked vase sitting on my window sill, the vase I broke and re-glued, well, it looks as pretty as ever.

I love the sense of family that never gives up on it's wounded members. That's Wabi-sabi at its highest and best practice. We all make a mess of things at times. But in a certain light, from a certain angle, we can see that grace still abides with us all, that forgiveness is like powdered gold in the glue of loving kindness.

SEVENTY-FOUR

A glued broken vase,
the full moon lights up my work—
cracks glow pure silver

I LIVE IN a cabin a little smaller than Thoreau's at Walden Pond. Mine's 9x12. At 108 square feet, it's about a third smaller than Henry David's.

Just inside the door, there's a piece of bamboo inscribed with lines from a Rumi poem: "A man who goes with half a loaf of bread to a small place that fits around him like a nest, someone who wants nothing more, who is himself not longed for by anyone, he is a letter to everyone. You open it. It says, Live."

A couple of things.

One thing, I have trouble with the phrase, *who is himself not longed for by anyone.* Sometimes I think I get it. I'll keep working on it. Which, I think, was Rumi's intent.

So, the other thing, the letter that I am, in my tiny home, is self-addressed with self-directed insights. Hail Polonius: To mine own self, it is my aim to be true. Like the priest I know who tells me every single one of his homilies is, first, a message to himself.

SEVENTY-FIVE

Big house, little house,
I have wandered through them all—
same size toilet bowls

EVERY TIME I am outside, and *present*, when I am mindful, and not chasing thoughts across other universes, I am rewarded by some small but magnificent act in nature's grand theater.

SEVENTY-SIX

Leaf chasing leaf down—
playful, like two birds falling,
they land side by side

SEVENTY-SEVEN

Woodsmoke rises straight,
damp air is still and cold tonight—
harvest moon looks warm

SEVENTY-EIGHT

Oak leaf floating by,
thin and narrow, ends turned up—
a viking's longboat

SEVENTY-NINE

Clouds follow the sun,
sunset horizon ablaze—
dog turds in the sand

EIGHTY

Smoke on the water,
early morning mist curling—
starry cold last night

EIGHTY-ONE

Young cypress assumes
character beyond its years—
river laughs quite near

I CALLED ON a friend one night in October, and the porch was decorated for Halloween. As I waited for her to answer the door, I noticed one of the carved pumpkins was dark among four or five others all aglow.

EIGHTY-TWO

Witches in the night,
pumpkins carved with funny faces—
moon behind a cloud

I Look In the mirror, and sometimes I'm surprised to see a man my age. What's even more surprising is when I act my age. When I was a kid, and wild as a buck, my age itself *was* the act.

Then I got a little older and found bars, and the act got a little rougher.

I don't fight any more. Or water ski. Or drive cars too fast. Or care very much that I don't have hair on the top part of my head.

I used to eat a lot of fried eggs and fried bacon, and fried hash browns.

EIGHTY-THREE

Oats and barley in a bowl
with strawberries, blueberries—
rum in my coffee

AND WHAT GIVES when the road abruptly ends and launches me into the void?

Tolstoy said, "When you think about what will happen to your soul after death, think also about what happened to your soul before your birth. If you plan to go somewhere, then you came from somewhere. Where do we go after death? We go to where we came from."

Rumi, in a poem adds, "Out beyond ideas of right doing and wrong doing, there is a field. I'll meet you there."

EIGHTY-FOUR

Old man sits on rock,
brave warrior long ago,
he counts rose petals

EIGHTY-FIVE

My soul dreaming peace:
little white church in the vail—
fast cars flying past

THIS MORNING, A sprinkling of clover at my feet. Each clover leaf was adorned with a single jeweled drop of dew. I got down on my knees. I put my palms on the ground and bent my face closer. One clover stood taller than the rest, like an elegant lady dressed up in a holy trinity of her finest diamonds.

At dusk, after the ball is over, the clover will sleep and fold its leaves like a tiny green angel, its jade wings at rest.

EIGHTY-SIX

Clover sleeps at night
relaxing leaves to her side—
stars fall, morning dew

WHEN I SAW the hawk, the starlings were moving in his direction, murmuring, flying together like gathered and drifting smoke across a harvested field of cotton, toward bellied power lines strung between bare poles like so many tall crosses in a row.

The raptor was a heavy dark spot in a small copse of gray trees on the edge of the field, and it reminded me of a cat that knows it has won the mouse and lays down for a minute to watch it struggle before the kill.

EIGHTY-SEVEN

Murmur of starlings,
flying together as one—
hawk stares from a branch

IT'S NEVER THIS or that. Always a little of both.

EIGHTY-EIGHT

Rain has moved on past
and sunlight towels wet leaves—
still, they drip, drip, drip

WE COOK UP ideas for how things will go, devise schemes to guide our progress, make a map for how to get there, and, alas, something doesn't quite work out the way we planned, possibly even better.

EIGHTY-NINE

Oars, rudders, sails—
shallow sand meets a deep keel:
footprints on the beach

NINETY

Days and days of rain,
soppy wet clouds keep us in,
lovers light a fire

NINETY-ONE

Two men in a boat,
the fish aren't biting today—
beer in the cooler

I HAD AN uncle, a farm-country man, who said he did not care if the price of syrup went up to a dollar a sop. Though he loved to drag a hot buttered biscuit through Golden Eagle syrup poured into a puddle on his plate, he said if his syrup got too expensive he reckoned he'd just be still with it, get by, one way or the other.

NINETY-TWO

Squirrel and squirrel
chasing, timbering, scolding—
bird sits light and still

KURT VONNEGUT JR. allowed the most damning revelation a writer can make about himself is not knowing the difference between what's boring and what's not boring.

But, there doesn't have to be a knife in the neck, blood on the floor and sirens bearing down. Try a little old-fashioned incongruity.

NINETY-THREE

Noisy table,
holiday family meal—
baby sound asleep

WHEN I WAS a sailor aboard the USS Intrepid, I was confronted with a piece of me that needs work still.

I was an electronics technician and walked into our shop one day around noon when several of the ETs were hanging around. A bunch of guys cutting up, noisy, laughing. We'd been on a six-month overseas cruise, and were finally cruising toward our homeport in Quonset Point, Rhode Island.

One of the guys with a big megaphone voice drowned out the din with, "There's Brewer! Let's see if he wants us to stop and worry about something." Everybody laughed. Somebody added, "Yeah, Brewer, what kind of catastrophe you looking forward to today?"

All the wisdom traditions say don't worry about tomorrow. "Be here now," said the late Ram Dass, 60s American guru and spiritual teacher. "Each day's got trouble enough," Jesus allowed.

I've made lots of progress. But, fifty-some years later I still sometimes let my mind run amok with how badly things *could* go.

NINETY-FOUR

> Cow with calf close by,
> she's watching for coyotes—
> bull blinks, chewing grass

For all of our very human endeavor there is a silent presence, which, even in its passivity, seems more powerful than all our locomotives and tall buildings.

NINETY-FIVE

Farmer works the land,
sailors on ships work at sea,
cosmos swirls above

CAN IT BE, that we all truly are God's children—no matter how far apart our circumstances?

NINETY-SIX

Daisies in a pot,
wildflowers sprinkling the field—
town and country kin

THE STORY OF Saul of Tarsus walking on the dusty road to Damascus is, to me, has at least one thing in common with the story of Siddhartha sitting underneath the Bodhi tree.

Both men were of one mind one minute, and the next minute were transformed by some immediate renewal of their minds, even getting new names in the switch, Paul and Buddha, respectively.

I am given hope that it's never too late, as I see clearly that I'm not *there* yet, but running out of road.

NINETY-SEVEN

Grace is not time-bound,
some say merely love-released—
a thief on the cross

ALL ALONG THE whole of the Gulf of Mexico's coastal crescent from New Orleans to Apalachicola, we've got live oaks. They are plentiful and squat the land, low and broad, with gnarly twisted trunks and furrowed bark like the hide of some ancient thunderous beasts.

They grow easily and the grandfathers and grandmothers of the live oaks spread their canopies wider than houses. Many of them have trunks the size of whole rooms. They are the Druidic royalty of of the backwood landscape and even guard bronze placques in Southern city parks.

They are regal and the rough-barked limbs of the mighty live oaks droop under their own weight, and dip close to the ground at two-thirds their hundred-foot reach. And the ends of those branches turn up toward the sky like the palms of some conjuring sorcerer, bedecked in sleeves of green resurrection ferns that get crispy brown and dead-looking, but by secret and archaic alchemy switch back to green when the rain comes.*

* From my novel, *The Widow and the Tree*

Walking down by Weeks Bay with my little dog, taking a brisk jaunt on a chilly afternoon one week from Christmas, I spy on a live oak's branches the bright red lichen that so often decorates their strong arms.

The red and the green—crucifixion and resurrection, the plot and storied final pages of our teacher Jesus, that opened with a heralded birth still celebrated two thousand years later. The season's blessings to us all.

NINETY-EIGHT

>Stout and sure live oak:
>sailing ships' stems ribs futtocks—
>mangers and crosses

ABOUT TWENTY-FIVE years ago, I attended the Oxford (Mississippi) Conference for the Book, and sat in an auditorium for a reading by Richard Flanagan, a Tasmanian writer whose debut novel *Death of a River Guide* had the literary world by the throat. He was joined on stage by two other authors.

The host announced that each author had 15 minutes. The first author took 15 minutes to set up his reading, then read for almost 20 minutes. Then Flanagan stood up to the mic, he looked to his left at the previous reader, and said, "I'm not going to the set this up." Then he looked out at the audience and added, "If I have to do that, then I've chosen the wrong thing to read."

Richard Flanagan read for three minutes and when he finished, I found myself right there in the second row, sitting between William Gay and Suzanne Kingsbury, stunned and emotional. I held my eyes wide open, unblinking, and my lips pulled tight, trying to maintain my composure. Flanagan's brief reading had crushed me, his words augering into my heart. William and

Suzanne were friends of mine. They saw me come undone. Neither said a thing.

And now I'm finishing up *Syllables Go By*, this collection of 99 haiku. A genuine haiku doesn't even carry a title like other poems, much less numbers and a narrative set-up. That's because this form is intended to be slippery, like gold fish in a garden pond, and the reader is supposed to catch its meaning without help.

But, borrowing from Basho's dabbling and fusing of forms, in his *Narrow Road to the Interior*, I have introduced each of these poems. I am hopeful that I have chosen not too many words to make them land within your reach.

NINETY-NINE

He's from Nazareth—
can any good come from there?
let's just send him back

Sonny Brewer is the author of *The Poet of Tolstoy Park*, and four other novels; a children's book; a self-help book; a book about Clarence Darrow; the editor of *Stories from the Blue Moon Café* anthology series, and *Don't Quit Your Day Job* anthology. He founded The Fairhope Center for Writing Arts, and was a bookseller at his Over the Transom Bookstore. *Syllables Go By* is Sonny's first book of poetry.

www.ingramcontent.com/pod-product-compliance
Lightning Source LLC
Chambersburg PA
CBHW021951290426
44108CB00012B/1021